This book is dedicated to the memory of my brother Jared who shared joy with us all through his boisterous laughter.

"Sometimes you will never know the value of a moment until it becomes a memory."
- Dr. Seuss

The HappyCamper Guidebook
Your Guide to a Happier Life
BETA Version 1.1
by Nicole A. Donnelly
with Aubrey Wursten and Pearl Klein
Design by Jennifer Harowicz

A Special Thanks to: Sara Donnelly, Anne Amstutz Hayes, Simon Harlinghausen, Marilyn King, Sam Horn, Nicholas Luff, Curtis Dunsdon, Brian Anderson, Amanda Bredlow, Shauna Herter, Anne Bruns, Shine Kelly, Amanda Anuraga, Lauren Lofano, Robert Murray, Andrea Garfield, Chris Dierkes, Steve Curtis, Kate Lawrence, Jason York, Kris & Gary Sheets, Beth Sheets, Michele and Chris Dollar, Sage Rice, Tirion Rice, Magnolia Dollar, Simon Sinek, Peter Chee & thinkspace.

©2015 by HappyCamper.world

No part of this publication may be reproduced, stored in a retrieval system, or transmitted in any from by any means, electronic, mechanical, photocopying, recording, or otherwise without written permission of the publisher.
For information regarding permission, write to HappyCamper.world,
936 N 34th Street, Suite 400, Seattle, WA 98103.
ISBN ISBN-10: 1-62676-942-7
ISBN-13: 978-1-62676-942-7
Published by HappyPress

NOURISHING 1 BILLION SOULS.
EMOTIONALLY. MENTALLY. PHYSICALLY. SPIRITUALLY.
For free downloads and more information please go to www.HappyCamper.world

HappyCamper **Guidebook**
TABLE OF CONTENTS

INTRODUCTION 1-2

HOW TO USE THE GUIDEBOOK 4

CONNECT: EVA + CLINGY 6

CREATE: OLIVER + FLIT 14

BUILD: ARI + BOSSY 22

HELP: JOHNNY + SHY 30

ACHIEVE: SONIA + BULLY 38

LEAD: GRACE + CLOWN 46

CONCLUSION 53

POSTER 58

When my daughter Sara was 7, she experienced the emotions we all feel: fear, anger, sadness, frustration. As her mom, my heart ached to take away her pain. Like everybody, Sara had to learn how to deal with all these big feelings that would come up seemingly out of nowhere.

That's how the HappyCamper poster began. From scrapbook paper I created a poster that has 6 monsters on it, showing the emotional needs that are not being met that bring those monsters out. Sara could go to the wall and point to the monster, identify with it, and we'd have a conversation about what was going on for her.

It was amazing how quickly her feelings shifted as if the monster no longer had the power over her.

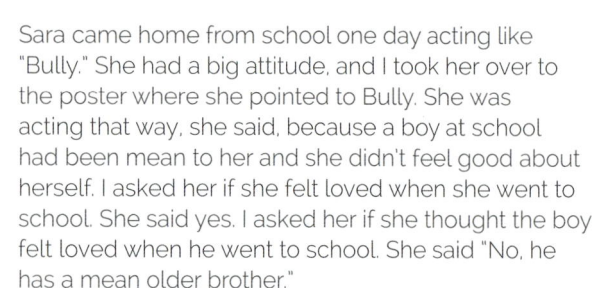

Sara came home from school one day acting like "Bully." She had a big attitude, and I took her over to the poster where she pointed to Bully. She was acting that way, she said, because a boy at school had been mean to her and she didn't feel good about herself. I asked her if she felt loved when she went to school. She said yes. I asked her if she thought the boy felt loved when he went to school. She said "No, he has a mean older brother."

We discussed how Sara would talk with the boy, not his monster. The next day, she went to school and talked to him as a person who is perfect, whole, and complete just as he is, not making him wrong for anything, and she disarmed the "Bully." Then they could get along as two happy kids.

These things don't happen only to kids. I remember once as a volunteer, I received a harsh email from another volunteer. I read it and felt sad and small. I was told I was doing a bad job, that I had 60 days to prove myself, and that the sender would be out of town for 30 days, so he wouldn't reply if I emailed him.

I took my HappyCamper poster down from the wall, put it on my desk, read it and thought about how I should respond. I identified the monsters that came out in the email and figured out how I could write a response that would speak to his emotional needs — not my anger that his needs triggered.

It took me about 10 days to come up with the right response to send. He replied within a few hours, apologized, and asked if we could meet when he was back in town.

In both of these relationships, Sara and I were finding our superpowers, the things we could do or say to feel happy and to create more HappyCampers in the world. *"Happiness is everybody's superpower," says Sara, "something everybody in the world can share with each other no matter how old you are!"*

Over the years Sara has consistently been frustrated that not everybody understands their monsters. She spreads the word to her friends as much as she can, and there are still millions of people out there who could use the HappyCamper poster.

In January of 2015, Sara and I made it our mission to give you the tools for creating empathy and compassion for yourself and for the ones you love.

OUR MISSION IS TO NOURISH 1 BILLION SOULS.

At the back of this book is your gift of the HappyCamper poster for your wall. Please download more copies at www.HappyCamper.world to share at your schools, library, YMCA, community center, after school programs, and church.

Keep this guidebook with you at home, in your backpack, at your desk — everywhere you go in life.

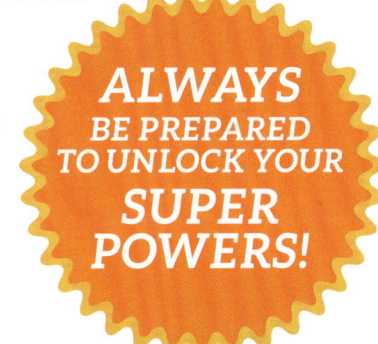

ALWAYS BE PREPARED TO UNLOCK YOUR SUPER POWERS!

"**Happiness** is everybody's superpower - it's something everybody in the world can share with each other."

- Sara

HOW TO USE THE
HappyCamper Guidebook

You have emotional superpowers. Some of them come naturally to you, and others you work harder to bring out. You are capable of dealing with your feelings, whether they are happy or challenging, and you can learn to make yourself stronger.

When you see how a monster shows up in you, you can get yourself back on the road to becoming a HappyCamper. And you can help other people see their own monsters so they can get themselves back to being HappyCampers.

If your monster is coming out, look at your monster in the book or on the poster and figure out what feelings are coming up. Take actions to disarm your own monster first, then others. There are phrases you can repeat to yourself, and there are ideas of what to say to others.

Read on to disarm your monsters and become a HappyCamper.

5 HAPPYCAMPER GROUND RULES:

#1 GET CURIOUS.

#2 NOBODY IS WRONG.
Everyone expresses their feelings differently.

#3 NO BLAME, NO EXCUSES.

#4 BE KIND.

#5 TAKE RESPONSIBILITY FOR YOURSELF.

"**Connection** is the energy that is created between people when they feel seen, heard, and valued."

– Brené Brown

MEET
Eva Clark
AND
CLINGY

EVA = CONNECT

Hi, I'm **EVA CLARK** and I love to connect with people.

WHEN I'M FEELING LOVED, I SAY THINGS LIKE:

Let's be friends. **OR** *Good job.* **OR** *You did great!* **OR** *I won't take it personally.* **OR** *Let's hang out, you'll love my friends.*

PLACE STICKER HERE

I FEEL RESPECTED WHEN:

- People say thank you.
- Somebody notices what I did for someone else and says so.

I'VE GOT YOUR BACK WHEN:

- Somebody says mean things about you.
- I promise to say only nice things about you.

{ *Tell a story about a time when you felt loved.* }

{ *How do you help others feel loved?* }

When I don't feel loved,
CLINGY comes out to get love.
“ *I feel sad and lonely — I'll do anything to make you love me.* ”

8

CLINGY

Hi, I'm **CLINGY** and I'll do anything to make you love me.

WHEN CLINGY COMES OUT, I SAY THINGS LIKE:

" *I'll do your homework.* **OR** *Give you my lunch money.* **OR** *You don't love me or care about me.* **OR** *I don't matter to you.* **OR** *I can do it myself!* **OR** *I'll buy you candy.* "

THINGS I DO WHEN I'M TRYING TO GET LOVE:

- ♥ Climb on your lap when you're working.
- ♥ Gossip about people who aren't around.

I FEEL UPSET WHEN:
- ♥ Nobody notices the nice things I do.

I DON'T HAVE YOUR BACK WHEN:
- ♥ Other people are gossiping and I join in or listen and don't stop it.

I MAKE PEOPLE WRONG BY:
- ♥ Blaming them for how I feel.
- ♥ Thinking they don't like me.

{ *Tell a story about a time when you felt unloved.* }

{ *How can you make yourself feel loved again?* }

HOW TO DISARM CLINGY

IN YOURSELF
REPEAT *"I am lovable"* 10 times out loud in the mirror.
REPEAT *"I belong"* 10 times out loud in the mirror.

IN OTHERS
Tell CLINGY *"Thank you"* for sharing or *"I appreciate your kindness"*.

"LET'S MAKE NEW FRIENDS"

NOW IT'S YOUR TURN!
Use the space below to write and draw your own scene.

"   "

12

> "It's kind of **fun** to do the impossible."
>
> – Walt Disney

MEET
Oliver Novak
AND
FLIT

OLIVER = CREATE

Hi, I'm **OLIVER NOVAK** and I love to have fun, explore, and discover new things.

WHEN I'M FEELING CREATIVE, I SAY THINGS LIKE:

" I have an idea. OR I can make this fun. OR Let's try again in a different way. OR Nothing because I'm so busy creating. "

PLACE STICKER HERE

I FEEL RESPECTED WHEN:

- People listen to my ideas.
- I am trusted to work independently.

I'VE GOT YOUR BACK WHEN:

- You are trying something new.
- I've got ideas for how you can do it — Just ask!

{ *Tell a story about a time when you felt creative.* }

{ *How do you help others feel creative?* }

When I don't feel challenged,
FLIT comes out to have fun.
"*I feel bored and distracted when I'm not doing anything new or fun.*"

FLIT

Hi, I'm **FLIT** and I want to have fun!

WHEN FLIT COMES OUT, I SAY THINGS LIKE:

" *Next.* **OR** *Whatever.* **OR** *I want to do something else.* **OR** *Everything is so boring.* **OR** *Nothing matters anyway!* **OR** *I don't care!* **OR** *You can't make me!* "

THINGS I DO WHEN I'M TRYING TO HAVE FUN:

- Change what I'm doing. Start something new.
- Walk away from what's not fun right now.

I FEEL UPSET WHEN:

- I'm told to finish something boring.
- People tell me something is more interesting than it is to me.

I DON'T HAVE YOUR BACK WHEN:

- You want me to do something with you that I'm already done with.

I MAKE PEOPLE WRONG BY:

- Saying what they are doing is boring, or not worth my time.
- Blaming them for how I feel.

{ *Tell a story about a time when you got distracted.* }

{ *How can you make your work fun?* }

HOW TO DISARM FLIT

IN YOURSELF
REPEAT *"I am free"* 10 times out loud in the mirror.
REPEAT *"I am fun"* 10 times out loud in the mirror.

IN OTHERS
Tell FLIT *"Thank you"* for sticking with a task until it's done.

"LET'S MAKE IT FUN."

Oliver's family has a rule that everyone has to help out, and it's his turn to do the dishes. He fills the sink with hot water and soap and has fun building towers of soap bubbles.

As he washes each dish, he pretends they are explosive. Nothing breaks!

NOW IT'S YOUR TURN!

Use the space below to write and draw your own scene.

"   "

20

"You cannot fail, you can only produce **results**."

– Wayne W. Dyer

MEET
Ari Russo
AND
BOSSY

ARI = BUILD

Hi, I'm **ARI RUSSO** and I love it when everything gets done the way I expected.

WHEN I'M FEELING PRODUCTIVE, I SAY THINGS LIKE:

❝ *We can do that.* **OR** *I like this idea, what do you think?* **OR** *This doesn't seem right to me, may we please do it a different way?* **OR** *You get to go first!* ❞

PLACE STICKER HERE

I FEEL RESPECTED WHEN:

🏠 People ask for my ideas about the best way to get something done.

🏠 I get to take my time getting things the way I want them.

I'VE GOT YOUR BACK WHEN:

🏠 You're trying to figure out how to make something work and feeling frustrated.

{ *Tell a story about a time when you were proud of what you made.* }

{ *How do you help others feel proud of making something?* }

When I don't feel productive,
BOSSY comes out to take control.

"*If we did things the way I said, we wouldn't be having these problems.*"

BOSSY

Hi, I'm **BOSSY** and I want you to do it my way!

WHEN BOSSY COMES OUT, I SAY THINGS LIKE:

Because I said so. **OR** *Do it my way.* **OR** *This is a stupid idea.* **OR** *Whatever — I guess you're the boss.* **OR** *Are you REALLY going to do that?*

THINGS I DO WHEN I'M TRYING TO BE IN CONTROL:

- Criticize how other people do things.
- Take over so I can make things turn out right.

I FEEL UPSET WHEN:
- Nobody pays attention to my plans and ideas.

I DON'T HAVE YOUR BACK WHEN:
- Your idea for getting something done doesn't make sense to me.

I MAKE PEOPLE WRONG BY:
- Telling them I know the right way to do something.

{ *Tell a story about a time when you didn't get things done.* }

{ *How can you make yourself feel in control?* }

HOW TO DISARM BOSSY

IN YOURSELF
REPEAT *"I am in control"* 10 times out loud in the mirror.
REPEAT *"I am okay"* 10 times out loud in the mirror.

IN OTHERS
Tell BOSSY *"Thank you"* for producing results, for making sure that things are getting done.

"LET'S START A LEMONADE STAND."

"I'm gonna start the best lemonade stand ever!"

The next day, he sets up a second table 2 blocks away.

"Hey, can I help with that?"

"Sure, as long as you do it my way."

Ari gets really organized, and on his very first day, he sells out in an hour.

His little sister is getting in the way riding her bike in circles. Ari is starting to get mad when he figures out the perfect job for her...

"Good job sis!"

She can go back and forth to the stands and tell him how business is going.

NOW IT'S YOUR TURN!

Use the space below to write and draw your own scene.

"   "

> "Encourage, lift, and strengthen one another. For the positive energy spread to one will be felt by all of us."

― Deborah Day

MEET
Johnny Kim
AND
SHY

JOHNNY = HELP

Hi, I'm **JOHNNY KIM** and I feel peace and stability when I help others and give them what they need.

WHEN I'M FEELING SUPPORTIVE, I SAY THINGS LIKE:

> *Let me give you a hand.* **OR** *I'm going to ask him if he wants to play, too.* **OR** *I'll help you with that.*

PLACE STICKER HERE

I FEEL RESPECTED WHEN:

- I get to decide how much time I spend alone or with others.

I'VE GOT YOUR BACK WHEN:

- You don't feel confident that you can get something done. You can count on me.

{ *Tell a story about a time when you were able to help others.* }

{ *How do you help others feel calm?* }

When I don't feel supportive,
SHY comes out to get peace and stability.
" *I will withdraw when I don't know how to give you support.* **"**

SHY

Hi, I'm **SHY** and I need my space.

WHEN SHY COMES OUT, I SAY THINGS LIKE:

I just want to stay home. **OR** *I don't have any friends.* **OR** *Everything is so stupid!* **OR** *I can't take it anymore! I don't want to be around you.*

THINGS I DO WHEN I'M TRYING TO GET PEACE AND STABILITY:

Go to my room and be by myself.

I FEEL UPSET WHEN:

- People around me aren't getting along.
- Someone is mad at me, or I think someone is.

I DON'T HAVE YOUR BACK WHEN:

- You're fighting with someone else — I'm outta there.

I MAKE PEOPLE WRONG BY:

- Not being okay when they disagree with each other.
- Avoiding conversations.

{ *Tell a story about a time when you felt stressed out by an argument.* }

{ *How can you make yourself feel calm?* }

HOW TO DISARM SHY

IN YOURSELF
REPEAT *"I am in control of myself"* 10 times out loud in the mirror.
REPEAT *"I am helpful"* 10 times out loud in the mirror.

IN OTHERS
Tell SHY *"Thank you"* for helping.

"LET'S HELP 100 PEOPLE TODAY."

Johnny is sorting out donated clothing at his church. It's winter and there are a 100 people who need winter coats.

How am I going to find enough coats for all those people? How are we ever going to get through all those boxes?

Overwhelmed, he stares at the enormous pile of boxes.

"Hey Oliver, let's race to 50 coats each!"

"You're on!"

As the pile of coats grows, Johnny feels good about supporting those in need.

NOW IT'S YOUR TURN!

Use the space below to write and draw your own scene.

"   "

> "Only those who dare to fail greatly can **achieve** greatly."
>
> – Robert F. Kennedy

MEET Sonia Cruz AND BULLY

SONIA = ACHIEVE

Hi, I'm **SONIA CRUZ** and I love feeling unique, important, and needed. I feel good when I'm able to be myself.

WHEN I'M ACHIEVING, I SAY THINGS LIKE:

" I do my best! **OR** *You can count on me.* **OR** *My team depends on me to play my hardest. "*

I FEEL RESPECTED WHEN:

★ People notice what I'm good at and give me the opportunity to do more of it.

I'VE GOT YOUR BACK WHEN:

★ Nobody else sees how hard you're trying but I do.

★ I celebrate you!

{ *Tell a story about a time when you felt really important.* }

{ *How do you help others feel proud of themselves?* }

When I don't feel successful, BULLY comes out to make me feel special.

" *It's easy to hurt my feelings when I don't feel like I'm able to do my best.* **"**

BULLY

Hi, I'm **BULLY** and I am better than you.

WHEN BULLY COMES OUT, I SAY THINGS LIKE:

❝ *I'm better than you.* **OR** *You're no good.* **OR** *The stupid ref lost the game for us.* **OR** *How could you make such a dumb mistake?* ❞

THINGS I DO WHEN I'M TRYING TO FEEL SPECIAL:

- ★ Tell everybody how stupid they are and put them down.
- ★ Be mean-funny.
- ★ Make fun of others.

I FEEL UPSET WHEN:

- ★ I try my best and still can't get it right.

I DON'T HAVE YOUR BACK WHEN:

- ★ I tell everyone about the dumb things you do.

I MAKE PEOPLE WRONG BY:

- ★ Blaming them for losing the game.
- ★ Blaming the teacher for giving me a bad grade.

{ *Tell a story about a time when you didn't feel important.* }

{ *How can you make yourself feel needed?* }

HOW TO DISARM BULLY

IN YOURSELF
REPEAT *"I am awesome"* 10 times out loud in the mirror.
REPEAT *"I do what I say I am going to do"* 10 times out loud in the mirror.

IN OTHERS
Tell BULLY *"Thank you"* for making a great play, for putting in a lot of effort, for doing what you say your going to do.

"LET'S WIN THE GAME!"

Halfway through warmups, frustrated, she stomps off to the bathroom. Sonia thinks about her team, and how she doesn't want to let them down.

She runs back outside and plays her best!

NOW IT'S YOUR TURN!

Use the space below to write and draw your own scene.

"   "

"Everyone you will ever meet knows something you don't."

– Bill Nye

MEET
Grace Washington
AND
CLOWN

GRACE = LEAD

Hi, I'm **GRACE WASHINGTON** and I love when I learn something new. I grow when I'm faced with a challenge and deal with it.

WHEN I'M LEADING, I SAY THINGS LIKE:

Let's do it. **OR** *I'll teach you how!* **OR** *Follow me!* **OR** *I can do that.* **OR** *We can figure that out.*

PLACE STICKER HERE

I FEEL RESPECTED WHEN:

- I get to lead the team or project.
- I am given responsibility I can rise to.

I'VE GOT YOUR BACK WHEN:

- Things get tough; we can figure it out together.
- It's no problem.

{ *Tell a story about a time when you felt like a leader.* }

{ *How do you help others learn and grow?* }

When I don't feel smart,
CLOWN comes out to get attention.

❝ *I feel ashamed when I don't know something, so I'll start making jokes and goofing off so people will laugh.* ❞

CLOWN

Hi, I'm **CLOWN** and I like to be silly.

WHEN CLOWN COMES OUT, I SAY THINGS LIKE:

" Look what I'm doing! **OR** *Did you hear the one about...?* **OR** *Look how good I am at this!* **OR** *Look at me! "*

THINGS I DO WHEN I'M TRYING TO FEEL ACCEPTED:

- Crack jokes, make up stories, tap-dance.
- Sing extra loud in the choir.

I FEEL UPSET WHEN:

- Somebody else gets the attention I know I deserve.

I DON'T HAVE YOUR BACK WHEN:

- I don't feel smart so I make fun of what you said or talk over you.

I MAKE PEOPLE WRONG BY:

- Making them feel small about their part.
- Making my point seem more important than theirs.

{ *Tell a story about a time when you didn't feel like a leader.* }

{ *How can you make yourself feel smart?* }

HOW TO DISARM CLOWN

IN YOURSELF
REPEAT *"I am thankful"* 10 times out loud in the mirror.
REPEAT *"I can learn"* 10 times out loud in the mirror.

IN OTHERS
Tell CLOWN *"Thank you"* for taking responsibility, leading others to success, for being entertaining.

50

"LET'S MAKE BEAUTIFUL SONGS TOGETHER."

Grace loves to sing in choir and always gets the solo, except for today.

HOW COME I DIDN'T GET THE SOLO!?!

Grace wants to sing louder than the other kids and chooses not to.

Grace felt proud of her choir when the parents raved about the performance.

NOW IT'S YOUR TURN!

Use the space below to write and draw your own scene.

"   "

52

You have great emotional superowers that you can call on to defeat your emotional monsters. When you bring out your superpowers, you'll get even better at bringing them out in others. You'll be able to see someone who is having a bad day and help them figure out how to make it better. You'll be able to stop fighting with friends and disarm bullies.

And we will be one step closer to living in a world with 1 billion people who know how to be and create HappyCampers!